Christmas

illustrated by
Lynne Armstrong

Starters Facts · Blue 4
Macdonald Educational

The days before Christmas
are called Advent.
This girl has an Advent calendar.
She opens a window
of the calendar each day.
On December 25th it will be Christmas day!

2

Bible

crib

At Christmas you can see a crib in the church.
Christmas is a special day for Christians.
They remember that Jesus was born
on Christmas day.
The story of the very first Christmas
is told in a book called the Bible.

3

A long, long time ago
there was a carpenter called Joseph.
His wife was called Mary.
They were visiting a town called Bethlehem.
Mary was going to have a baby.
She had been told it was the Son of God.

4

Bethlehem was full of people.
Joseph and Mary could not find
anywhere to stay.
All the inns were full.
The only place they could find
was a stable.

Not far away, some shepherds
were looking after their sheep.
They saw a bright light in the sky.
They thought they could hear voices of angels
telling them to go to Bethlehem.

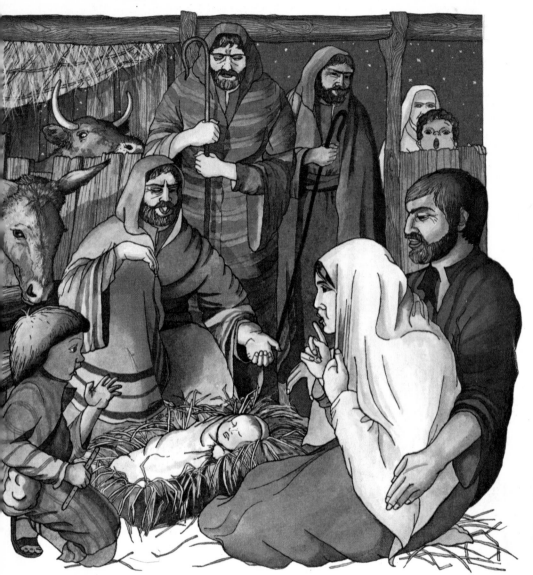

They ran to the stable.
There they found Mary and Joseph
with the baby Jesus.

Today we have a holiday at Christmas time.
Even before Jesus was born
there were winter holidays.
The Romans had a holiday.
They gave presents and had parties,
just like we do at Christmas.

8

In northern lands the
winter nights were dark and cold.
The winter holiday was called Yule.
People lit big bonfires at Yule time.
They liked to dance and sing.

paper
chain

holly

At Christmas time we like to
decorate our houses.
We put up holly and mistletoe.
We make paper chains.

10

mistletoe

Christmas
tree

Presents are put round
the Christmas tree.

In many countries,
carol singers go from house to house.
They stand outside in the cold
and sing Christmas Carols.

In Mexico it is hot at Christmas.
People decorate their houses.
Inside the coloured star there are
little presents for the children.

We all know Santa Claus.
In Holland he visits children
on December the 5th.
If they have been good,
he gives them presents.

In Britain and America, they say
that Santa drives a sleigh.
Reindeers pull the sleigh
across the sky.

These children have hung up their stockings.
Santa has filled them with presents.

In Australia, Christmas Day
is hot and sunny.
People can eat their dinner
sitting on the beach.

On the last day of December
it is New Year's Eve.
In Scotland this is called Hogmanay.
If a man comes through the door
just after midnight,
he brings good luck to the house.

The Chinese New Year
is on a different day each year.
The Chinese let off fireworks
and dance with paper dragons.

After New Year's Day comes Epiphany
Epiphany is on January 6th.
At Epiphany Christians remember
the three kings.
They followed a star to Bethlehem.
There they found the baby Jesus
and gave him presents.

In France, at Epiphany,
people eat a special cake.
In the cake is a bean.
This girl has found the bean.
She is crowned queen,
and can choose her king.

Christmas Activity

The carol singers hold a lantern
to see the words in the book.
You can make a pretend lantern
to hang up on the Christmas tree.

1. Take a piece of paper this shape. Colour it on both sides. Cut off a strip.

2. Fold the paper in half lengthways.

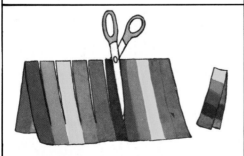

3. Cut slits in the paper as shown.

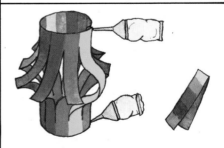

4. Open up the paper and glue as shown.

5. Stick on the paper strip for a handle.

Christmas Quiz

At Christmas we send cards
to our friends.
This Christmas card
shows the baby Jesus.

What was His mother called?
Which town was He born in?
How many kings came to see Him?

Christmas Puzzle

Look at all the presents.
We must put them round the tree.
There are two of each.
How many pairs can you see?

ChristmasWordList

Advent calendar page 2 	lantern page 12 
crib page 3 	sleigh page 15 
Yule page 9 	presents page 17 
holly page 10 	Christmas dinner page 18 
Christmas tree page 11 	Epiphany page 22